To You Who Don't Understand,

To You Who Don't Understand,

Naomi-Nicole F. E. Bramer

LIFE RATTLE PRESS

To You Who Don't Understand,

Published by Life Rattle Press
Toronto, Canada
Life Rattle New Writers Series

Copyright © by 2017 Naomi-Nicole F.E. Bramer

All rights reserved. The use of any part of this publication reproduced, transmitted in any form or by any means, electronic, mechanical, photocopying, recording or otherwise, or stored in a retrieval system, without the prior consent of the author is an infringement on the copyright law.

ISBN 978-1-987936-30-8

Copy Edited by Jade Garrido
Stories Edited by Emily Karim
Cover Art by Maiko Goshima
Cover Work by Takayuki Maruyama

For all the fighters living with depression. You are brave, you are strong, you are wonderful. We got this.

For all the fighters helping us with depression. You are needed, you are wanted, you are appreciated. Thank you.

Come to me, all you who are weary and burdened, and I will give you rest.

Matthew 11:18

Table Of Contents

Introduction i

Part One: Depression
    Grey 1
    Shadow Man 2
    Too Much................................. 5
    Nothingness 6
    Untold Story........................... 10
    In My Mind 11
    Watch me Drown 16
    Good-bye 17
    Science Fair, Boobs, and Judgements ... 18
    In the Shadows 24
    Chemical Imbalances 25
    Is it my Fault? 29
    I am not my Depression 30

Part Two: Losing Control
    I'm Tired 35
    Acrostic Poem 36
    Crimson River 37

The World Goes Black 41
Break Free 42
Don't Take it Personally 43
Never to Forget 45
The Pain 47
Castle of Blankets 48
Erosion. 53
I Don't Want to Feel Anymore 54
Second Chances 55

Part Three: Learning to Cope
Fly With Me to Neverland 61
Mary 63
Some Advice to Help 66
Enough 69
How to Choose Your Words Wisely Pt.1 ... 71
You Are You 74
My Prayer, My Plea 75
Battles 76
How to Choose Your Words Wisely Pt.2 ... 77
Office Hours 80
Will You? 85
I'm Fine 86
Today is a Good Day 88

Living with Depression v

Acknowledgments ix

Introduction

I have depression. There. I said it. I never thought I would openly admit my mental illness to the world. Heck, I never thought I would write a book about it. But I am. And I did. And I did it all for one reason: because just maybe, this will help someone.

First, let me tell you what this book is not. It is not a self-help book. If you suffer from depression (or suspect that you do), I really do wish this book could help you, but it probably won't. I can't offer any great insight into how to get over depression; I still battle with the illness myself. It is not an autobiography. This is not a chronicle of my life, or even of my daily struggle with depression. I'm not that interesting. It is not a book that will tell you exactly what to do or what to say when dealing with a loved one who has depression. No one can do that. Depression affects every one differently, what works to help and comfort one person may not work for another. Even things that may have worked for someone

To You Who Don't Understand,

one time, may not work again. Difficult huh? But this is one of the reasons I decided to write this book.

Now, let me tell you what this book is. It is a collection of my creative non-fiction short stories, letters and poems all dealing with the topic of depression. Why? I wrote it for those of you who may have family or friends who suffer, not only from depression, but any form of mental illness. I wrote it so that maybe you can try to understand what we are going though. I wrote it so that maybe you could learn to be patient. Because mental illnesses affect us all!

I was diaognosed with Severe Unipolar Depression. Better known as, depression. I was fifteen years old. Since then, propelled by my love of writing and the advice of a guidance counsellor, I continued (rather inconsistently) to record my thoughts, feelings and struggles. This book is a collection of those records. Some pieces found within these pages were written over ten years ago, some were written ten days ago. I didn't share them to be judged on the skill of my writing, but to give an inside look at my mind. The mind of someone who lives with depression.

The idea for this book started from a letter I wrote. The letter, found in this collection under the title "Nothingness," was written partially out of frustration, partially out of hope. Frustration, that so many people in my lilfe did not seem to understand what it was like for myself, or anyone else, living with depression. Hope, that maybe the letter could help them understand, just a little, what it felt like to struggle with a mental illness.

I used to be very hesitant to admit my depression to anyone because of the stigma connected with mental illnesses. I was worried people would judge me. It took somebody close to me going through a similar experience to mine that made me realise, if I could be a bit more open about my problems, maybe I can help someone. And one of the biggest problems that people with depression voice is that, "no one understands."

My hope for this book is to help people who have loved ones suffering from depression, or any other mental illness. I want them to recognize just what we might be going through. And maybe bridge the gap of understanding - if only even a little.

Part One: Depression

Depression

Grey

My life is a billow of smoke
A whirlwind of grey haze
Upon this ash and dust, I choke
My fate 'til end of days

To You Who Don't Understand,

Shadow Man

There's a man that follows behind me.

Everywhere I go. Stalking me. He's darker than the shadows, so I know that he is always there. Even in the darkest of nights. In fact, in the dimmest of nights I see his presence even more, using the cover of emptiness and darkness to lurk closer to me. I cannot see him clearly, yet I know he is there. His silhouette, my shadow. Whether I'm tucked into bed waiting for sleep to greet me, or walking down the sidewalk preparing to take on the day, he's there.

The man that follows behind me.

When I go for a walk, to feel the breeze against my skin, I can feel him following behind me. His steps matching the rhythm of mine. I stop, he stops. I run, he runs. Sometimes he follows far behind and I can forget his presence for a while. I can live life the way I know life should be lived. Sometimes he sticks close to me, dragging me down. Making it difficult to carry on with a normal life. These are the worst days;

when he acts as my shadow and attaches himself to me, like Wendy sewing Peter Pan's shadow to his feet. Every step I take, he takes with me. Everywhere I go, he's there.

The man that follows behind me.

When I must attend class, or go to the library to study, I can feel him standing beside me. He tries to push his presence into my mind, making it difficult to concentrate. The darkness that surrounds him, that is him, creeps over me. Covers me in a blanket of wispy blackness, seemingly weightless yet threatening to crush me. He pulls the hazy darkness over my eyes, creating a veil that distorts and blurs everything I see. Nothing is as it seems anymore. Everything I do, he twists and alters.

The man that follows behind me.

When I get ready to go out, for work or just with friends, I can feel him staring at me through judging eyes. He leans in close and I can hear him whisper in my ear, criticizing me. Breathing disapprovals down my neck. He tells me I'm not pretty enough. That my eyes are too small, my cheekbones too high, my lips too red. He laughs at my height and pokes fun at my weight. He strokes my conscious with his vile words, slowly poisoning me. He taunts and teases until I believe him. Everything I think, he insults.

The man that follows behind me.

The exhaustion of fighting him off can occasionally be too much. So sometimes I give in to him. Let him envelope

To You Who Don't Understand,

me in his darkness. At times it's simpler this way, letting him embrace me. It's comfortable even. I feel nothing when I am tangled up with him. No pain, no frustration, no judgement. We lie together, him and I, dead to everything else in the world. We are in our own world. He whispers for me to join him in this world forever. Caressing me to leave reality behind. But I know his words and this world, are just a trap. If I leave my world behind, there is no going back. But unravelling myself from him is the hardest battle I must fight, his arms an iron cage.

I cannot escape him. As long as I am living he is there. The man that follows behind me. My depression that won't leave me alone.

Depression

Too Much

If I could rip out my heart and stop feeling
I would
The pulse, the beat, the pain
All together
Too much

To You Who Don't Understand,

Nothingness

To You Who Don't Understand,

I mean no offense. I meant that in the nicest way possible, which is why I write you this letter. To maybe help you understand, even if just a little bit better. But for all of us who do understand, who must live with the experience, I will try to explain it on our behalf. And so, You Who Do Not Understand, I write this letter to you.

Depression is one of the most common illnesses in the world. Yes, it is an illness, just like diabetes, AIDS or cancer. And no, there's no cure, though there are many "treatments" out there. Whether these treatments work vary from person to person, just like other medicine for other illnesses. What may work for one person is not guaranteed to work for another. And yes, sometimes there are good days, and sometimes there are bad days. But you may already know all this.

But if depression is one of the most common illnesses in the world, why do so many people still not understand?

Awareness is out there, yes. Articles and pictures and songs, speaking out about depression. People know it exists. But that's all it is. Everyone knows. Few understand. Truly understand. Which that in itself is understandable. Can anyone truly understand depression if they've never experienced it?

"Wait," you may think, "I understand, I've experienced depression once!" So many people assume they understand. "My significant other left me," "Someone close to me died," "I lost my job," and the list goes on. For all these reasons, and more, you may claim to have experienced "depression". For all the sorrow and hardships in life that have come your way, I am truly sorry. I too know the deep sorrow of loss. But that, and the depression I speak of here, are very different.

Unfortunately, the English language doesn't have a good enough word to fully describe the experience people living with depression face. In all those life experiences, the underlying factor of that depression is the feeling of sadness. People living with depression are often devoid of even this sadness that most people seem to think is synonymous with depression. The word sadness is only used because there is no other word in the English language that comes close to describing what we feel. But depression is devoid of sadness. It is devoid of everything. There is often no sadness or happiness or anger or feelings. There is nothing.

This "nothingness" weighs down on you until it becomes

To You Who Don't Understand,

your everything. The "nothingness" lies heavily on your body, causing real physical pain. A real physical pain that, because the origins are hard to locate, is difficult to treat. It is a real, physical pain that persists without ceasing. Migraines, severe back pain, muscle aches, joint pain, digestive problems, and chest pain can all be the reality of us who live with depression. And no, it's not all in our head. It's real. The pain is real. It's a reason drug, alcohol and self-inflicted abuse can run so rampant with us who suffer. Now, that is not meant to be an excuse, nor is it a suggestion to condone such actions. Rather, I say this to shed a little light, so maybe you can understand where we are coming from. If you were in a great deal of pain, continuously, without end, without relief, would you not try anything that could relieve you? Even if just a little? Even if just for a short while?

This "nothingness" also weighs down on your energy, until even the littlest tasks like getting out of bed seem impossible. Like a person suffering from a fever or the flu, fatigue takes over. It's not just something that we can "snap out of". The fatigue runs so deep into our bones that moving requires way more energy than our bodies can produce. Imagine walking to the bathroom with one-hundred pounds strapped to each foot. Not so easy, exhausting even. We have days where simply walking to the bathroom requires as much energy and effort as some people take to run a whole marathon. And like those who suffer from fatigue due to any other illnesses, we can't just "shake it off".

And worse yet, this "nothingness" weighs down on your mind, until it too is full of "nothing". One of the most common ways people living with depression describe what it feels like to others, is "drowning." It feels like we are drowning. Like something is closing in on us from all around, and it gets more and more difficult to breathe. Literally. Every breath is a battle we have to fight to take. This "nothingness" becomes your everything. And how do you get away from nothing?

I will end this letter with a quote from an article titled "What I Wish People Knew About Depression", by Therese Borchard: "I wish people knew that the hardest thing some persons will ever do in this lifetime is to stay alive, that just because staying alive comes easily to some, it doesn't mean arriving at a natural death is any less triumph for those who have to work so very hard to keep breathing."

Sincerely,

Someone Who Wishes You Understood (if only even a little)

To You Who Don't Understand,

Untold Story

Upon withered fruitless vine lies my dreams
Bird with broken wing, never to take flight
Now a barren wasteland my time does seem
My life forever more in moral plight
No more live night by night, nor day by day
Henceforth, you shall see me joyous no more
Engulfed in black night which does take away
All my hope; now I stand at sorrow's door
Flames within my soul dimmed and no more shines
Within darkest pit of dismay I lie
For comfort and happiness my heart pines
Oh woe, I have no more tears left to cry
    Through the depths of time secrets will unfold
    But alas, my story will go untold

In My Mind

"I'm so glad my best friend's hot!" Miko says while she separates another one-inch chunk of my hair and wraps it around the hot metal of the curling iron.

Ya right. She has to say that. She's my best friend.

I look into the large bathroom mirror, my dark brown eyes staring back at me. Plain eyes. Plain hair. Plain smile. Plain. Maybe not ugly, but definitely not pretty.

Why do I keep looking? Will some miracle happen and make me magically appear better the next time I look at my reflection?

"I think we should just leave your hair loose and let the curls cascade down," Miko states.

Ya, maybe that way it'll cover my face.

"Sure, I think it'll look better that way," I answer.

Miko sprays a finishing burst of hair spray on my fresh curls before she turns her attention and the curling iron to her own hair. Miko's light highlights look like caramel in her chocolate hued hair.

I check myself out in the mirror again. Springy curls hang below my shoulders.

Why do I keep looking? Did I think curly hair would look any different from when I have straight hair?

I pick up the eyeshadow palette and surf the multitude of colours. I choose a soft silver shade and tap the brush lightly through the pigment before sweeping the minerals across my left eyelid. I glance into the mirror to observe my handiwork. Freckles overshadow the shimmering silver on my eyelids. My freckles. They look like stains splattered sparsely across my nose and cheeks, like someone took dark paint and flicked it across my face. I always hated my freckles growing up. Whenever I went outside I would attempt to cover my nose and cheeks to avoid the sun exposure that would call forth my freckles.

Maybe I should just cover my face all the time.

I sweep the silver across my other eyelid before dipping the brush into a darker shade of grey. Light eyeshadow on the inside, darker on the outside. A little trick I learned to make my almond shaped eyes look bigger.

I can put on all the makeup I want but it will never be enough to actually make me pretty.

"What time is Selene getting here?" Miko asks.

"According to her text message, soon. She'll be completely ready to go though, so we should get changed now."

"Ok, I'm just finishing up my last few curls," Miko says. She unwinds her hair from the curling wand letting another curl bounce perfectly to her shoulders.

I pick out the pink tube of mascara from my makeup bag and turn to look at the mirror yet again.

Why do I keep looking? Will I ever learn my lesson to just stop looking?

I swipe on layer after layer of mascara, wishing my eyelashes were longer, thicker. I wished the eyes that stared back at me were completely different. I wished my entire face was different. Better. I throw the mascara on the counter and turn away from the mirror. I reach for the forest green halter top.

"Are you sure you don't want to wear a dress? You can borrow one of mine," Miko says glancing over at me.

I can't pull off those sexy dresses you and Selene wear.

"Nah," I answer as I pull the shirt over my head, careful not to mess up my curls or mascara, "I think short shorts and a backless halter top are sexy enough for me."

Probably too sexy for me.

I turn to Miko and hold my arms up in a shrug as she gazes over me, observing me from head to toe.

Say it. Say what we're both thinking. It's not good enough.

"You look hot," she declares, and turns to pull her slinky brown dress up her body.

I turn to study myself in the mirror one last time.

To You Who Don't Understand,

Not enough. I look too skinny. My boobs look too big. What am I, a stick with boobs? What kind of body am I trying to show off in this outfit? She just said that because she has to.

"How do I look?" Miko asks. She does a slow turn so I can see her from a 360-degree angle, "Don't my boobs look fantastic in this dress?"

"Ya, your cleavage is amazing," I laugh, "You look drop dead gorgeous."

I'll never look as good as her. No matter how hard I try, I will never be at her level.

The phone buzzes in my hand.

"Selene is here, let's go!" I inform Miko.

"Woot! Party! Let's do this!"

We dance to the front door and swing it open. Selene stands there in her short, beige dress. She leans on one leg with a hand on her hip. Her petite mouth turns up in a smile and reveals her perfect white teeth.

"Damn girl, you look fine!" Miko exclaims as she gives Selene the once-over.

"Aw, thanks hun," Selene throws her head back slightly and laughs delicately, "you guys look great too!"

I take in the scene before me. My two best friends. Gorgeous best friends. Flawless.

Why am I here? I don't fit in with them. I'm like the ugly best friend desperately trying to look as good as them. What a joke.

"Alright let's do this!" cries Miko.

Inside Guvernment, my eyes adjust to the dimness of the club as the three of us weave our way through the crowd of dancing bodies. We station ourselves at the far end of the bar.

"Alright, who wants to get us our first round of drinks?" Selene laughs.

If I tried I'd fail.

"Don't worry, I've got this," Miko says confidently.

And she does have this. I've never met anyone who can get guys to do anything the way she can. Guys flock to her. And Selene. Just as they were about to now. The group of guys Miko had just eyeballed were already making their way towards us. A simple smile and toss of her hair was all it took to reel them in. Now a group of guys stand in front of us, eager to buy us all drinks.

"Hey, what's your name?" A tall slim guy with curly dark hair flashes a grin at me.

He's definitely not into me. He's hitting on me to get to Miko or Selene. It's definitely not me he wants.

"My name's Coco," I answer.

He looks straight into my eyes and smiles, "Well Coco, can I buy you a drink?"

To You Who Don't Understand,

Watch me drown

    I will rely on no one but myself.

    I can rely on no one but myself.

    They can't help you. They will only ever let you down.

    I asked you to help save me, and you told me that you would.

    Yet, where are you in the hour of my need?

    I asked you to help save me,

    And you told me that you'd be there.

    I guess you meant to just watch me drown.

Good-bye

Standing here, sad, alone
Fun times now, overthrown
Never again to see your face
No more to hold in warm embrace

Left a piece of my heart
With you, when we did part
But all my feelings I bestow
Hear me whisper when wind doth blow

My last time by your side
Mute, though inside I cried
Sad as I am, I must still try
To say the saddest word… good-bye

To You Who Don't Understand,

Science Fair, Boobs, and Judgements

I run down the stark white tiled hallway on the main floor of my cousin's house, using my socks as skates to slide the rest of the way into the living room. Squeezing through the cramped together bodies of my aunts, uncles, cousins, nieces and nephews, I make my way to the kitchen. It's loud. My family parties are always loud. Loud and hot. Over a hundred bodies squished onto three floors of a single house will definitely raise the volume and temperature. I catch my breath as I grab a white styrofoam cup from the counter and pour lukewarm Cream Soda to the top. I wait for the bubbles to settle a little. I don't like carbonation. I drink half of the sweet pink liquid before making my way back through the crowd. I hold the drink to my chest making sure it doesn't spills down my favourite blue hoodie.

"Anak, come here," Mom calls out the pet name as she reaches out to take my hand.

She pulls me onto display in front of a group of her sisters.

Not all of them - there's too many to have them all together at once - but a bunch of them. They sit there, staring up at me expectantly.

"She won the science fair again," my mom says, and then adds, "we almost thought she wouldn't, but she did win last year in grade six as well. But there were a lot of good projects this year."

My aunts ooh and ahh for about one second before they talk about their own kids, and all their shining achievements, as if my presence somehow dissipated into the crowd. I back away slowly before slipping to freedom down the hallway.

I abandon my white Styrofoam cup full of pink cream soda on the brown hallway table. I bound up the stairs holding onto the rails so my short legs don't miss a step. But I still take a fantastic tumble down the entire flight of stairs. Nobody comes to help.

"Coco!" Anie leans over the railing at the top of the stairs.

I turn my neck upwards to see my cousin, with her shiny, honey hued hair falling over her large brown eyes. She flashes her straight-toothed smile.

"Hurry up!" she calls before disappearing into her sister's bedroom.

I bound up the stairs two at a time. *Ha! Take that stairs, I can master you.* I open the door to the room Anie had disappeared into seconds earlier. A group of my perfectly groomed older cousins sit on the double bed in the far corner.

To You Who Don't Understand,

I know my cousins are all gorgeous, not just because I think so but because random people would always say they are. People at church always compliment them. Their hair, their lips, their bodies. Random guys would come and flirt with them whenever we're all out. They are definitely a better-looking group of girls than average. The white canopy bed frame warps inward at the weight of so many girls resting at once. I turn in the opposite direction, towards my cousins with less makeup and less years of life. Crossing my legs, I plop down onto the grey carpeted floor amidst the girls my age. There's six of us in total, plus two honorary members who are just slightly younger and sometimes get the privilege of hanging out with us. We call ourselves the ESC. Only the eight of us know what it stands for but we're proud of our safe little girls group.

"Coco! Anie! Come here," my older cousin Hope waves us to the overcrowded bed.

Anie and I glance at each other. As the two eldest of the ESC, were we being invited over to the older cousins hang out? It was like being invited to the cool table in a school cafeteria. We both stand up, ready for our initiation. I look at Hope as we make our way across the room.

Last year Hope told me she'd buy me a bikini. A pretty red one. She said it would look good on me. I never did get a bikini.

Anie and I position ourselves to stand at the edge of the

bed. A group of eyes look at us. We stand and await our judgement.

"How big are your boobs?" Gemma finally breaks the silence.

I crinkle my nose. My boobs?

"Like, what size bra do you wear now?" Sierra clarifies.

"Um, a B?" Anie giggles, more in a question then a statement.

All eyes on me, expectantly.

"Um, my bra right now is a D…" I trail off.

"Oh, I knew it!" Hope exclaims, "You do have big boobs under those baggy sweaters."

Without hesitation, she hops off the bed and pulls the hem of my sweater up over my face.

"Wow. How do you have boobs that size on such a skinny body?" Emma asks.

"I dunno," I say through my sweater, Hope still holding it up over my face, "from my mom?"

I manage to pull my sweater out of Hopes hand and back down to cover my stomach and my boobs.

"Isn't it a little disproportionate?" Gemma says.

"Well, it's not like big boobs aren't a good thing." Angel argues.

"But Anie's boob size matches the rest of her body."

My pretty girl cousins continue to argue over big boobs and balanced bodies. Anie and I side glance at each other. We

To You Who Don't Understand,

aren't needed anymore in this conversation. We walk away. The other ESC members left the room already, probably to get more from the never-ending food supply. We bound down the first flight of stairs, slide across the tiles, then jog down the second set of stairs until we are in the crowded, unfinished basement. Metal folding chairs line the exposed plastic-covered fiberglass insulation. My much older cousins take up most of these seats. Most of these cousins are married with kids. Some members of the ESC's parents fall in this group. They are my cousins, yet closer to my mother's age than mine. That happens when your grandmother has twelve kids, and the oldest one starts having children while the youngest of the siblings is just born.

"Coco, Anie," our names are called again, this time by our older cousin Apple. She's sitting with Melody and Rachel. We walk over, bridging the gap between us and them. Standing in front of the chairs lined against the wall, we wait in front of our panel of judges.

"What grade are you guys in now?" Rachel asks.

"Seven," Anie and I answer in unison.

"So you're almost teenagers," Apple states.

I nod.

"You're all growing so fast," Rachel says.

I nod again, already bored of this conversation. I turn my head to signal Anie 'lets go'. She already got away. I look back to my cousins, smile and turn to walk away. I get about two chairs ahead before another aunt stops me. It's not far enough. I can still hear my cousin voices clearly. Their words are piercing.

"Anie will be taller too, and more slim. She'll look like a model. Too bad for Coco."

"Well, Anie is prettier than Coco."

Before my aunt can say anything to me, I turn and flee out of the basement. Wedging myself between the swarming bodies, I work to lose myself in the crowd.

To You Who Don't Understand,

In the Shadows

In the shadows I remain
Unable to measure up
I stare in wonderment, just like all the others,
At their extraordinary features
Captivating everyone, everywhere they go
Commanding men at the flick of a hand
Leaving me to stare on
In my eyes, jealousy and revel
In my heart, envy and inadequacy
Their beauty brings tears to my eyes
Not because of their appearance,
But more because of mine
Will this ugly duckling ever become a swan?
Or am I one already and I still can't measure up?
And so, I take another step back
So I won't be compared
But then I end up in your shadows once again

Chemical Imbalances

"Anata no koto ga suki na no ni. Watashi ni marude kyoumi nai…"

The upbeat music from my favourite J-pop group echoes in the small basement. I stare as the group of twenty or so bubbly girls in their matching blue, red, yellow and white outfits dance across my TV screen. Their smiles remain perfect as they sing about preparing themselves for heartbreak.

I should do that. I should put a smile on. There's no reason to be like this. Come on, just get up.

I pull my fuzzy grey blanket up closer to my neck and sink lower into the deceivingly uncomfortable black couch. The pile of paperwork on the coffee table lay untouched. I pass them a fleeting glance before closing my eyes and losing myself in the familiar spirited sounds of AKB48. As if beckoned by my thought of untouched business, Rintaro bounds his way into the space.

"Did you place that order on chopsticks yet?" he asks.

I open my eyes slowly and without moving my head, bring my gaze up to meet his. He knows I haven't done what he's asking. Our shared business email would have notified him if I had.

Just answer him. Come on, just say something. He's waiting.

"Not yet," I answer.

"When will you do it?" he persists.

"Soon."

He sighs as he pushes his long dark hair out of his eyes. We've been through this before.

"Why are you being like this?" Rintaro's voice rises.

He still doesn't understand. Please don't talk to me like that. Just breathe. It's not his fault. How can I explain this to him? Why can't I get up? Just get up.

I close my eyes against the pressure forming in the center of my forehead. I pause before I answer, "I'm not having a good day."

"You didn't even do anything," he points out.

"I got out of bed," I respond, my voice quiet and eyes still shut.

That's right. I got out of bed. You're doing ok. Just tell him you're doing ok. Just sit up.

"What?"

"I said, I got out of bed."

I force myself into a half sitting position before opening my eyes. Our eyes meet. I can see the furrow forming between his eyebrows. I try to steel myself for another argument. An argument that will take what little energy I have left. I look down at my fuzzy grey blanket.

"I'm sorry," I mutter, "I just feel… exhausted, ok?"

"You just need to force yourself to get up."

"I can't."

Don't let it get to you. Don't let it consume you. Get up. Just get up. It's not you. You're ok, just get up.

"You're a strong girl, just fight it. It's all in your mind."

I can hear the frustration in every word Rintaro says. I pinch the bridge of my nose in an attempt to reset my mind. A sigh escapes my lips.

That's right, fight it. This is nothing. Can he help me fight it? Just get up, you can do this. No big deal.

"So what if it's in my mind? Why does that mean it shouldn't affect me the way physical things do?"

Why doesn't he understand? Please understand. Why can't I make myself care enough to get up? This is important. I need to get this work done. I'm fighting with him again. Why can't I just get up?

"Because you're reacting to something that doesn't even exist in the real world!"

"People react to dreams. They wake up scared, or sad or happy. You can't say dreams aren't real."

To You Who Don't Understand,

"That's different! People have no control over their dreams."

"Are you saying I can control this?" I pause before adding, "I don't like feeling this way you know."

That's right. Why am I feeling this way? There's no reason to be like this. You can do this. Get up. Just get a few things done. Come on, don't let it consume you.

"You should still try."

"This *is* me trying."

He doesn't answer. We stay staring at each other in silence, neither of us having anything new to add to this played out conversation. He brushes the hair out of his face, giving me one last look before leaving the room.

Don't let him walk away. Please don't walk away. Wait. Come on, get up. Don't leave me here alone. Don't let it consume you. Why can't I get up?

I sink back into the straight-backed, hard black couch and pull my fuzzy, grey blanket up to my neck. My eyes glaze over as the cheerful sound of J-pop fills the basement room once again.

Is It My Fault?

Is it my fault,
That I can never make these things work?
What more can I do?
Do I not do enough? Say enough? Give enough?
Am I not enough?
Yet again, I'm forced to walk away
Or be left dangling
Waiting
Waiting for something more
Please tell me that this is not it for me
My heart can't take much more

To You Who Don't Understand,

I Am Not My Depression

To You Who Don't Understand,

I am not my depression. My depression is not me. Sometimes it may seem this way, but that's not the case. This is something I really want you make an effort to understand, so I will try my best to explain it to you. It's true that at times it consumes me. Clouds my thoughts and affects my actions. Sometimes it covers me so completely that it may seem like me and depression are one. But I am not my depression, and my depression is not me.

I am still me. There are still things that I like and things that I dislike. Things that I enjoy doing. But sometimes, my depression will make the things I like seem less enjoyable for awhile. And so, even though I know I still like something, I may not be interested in doing anything related to it. Sometimes my favourite hobbies will get pushed aside. It's still my favourite, but depression has made it so I can't enjoy it. So I may put it away briefly. Because nothing is fun when you have to force yourself too hard.

I'm not saying don't try to get me involved. Please know I always appreciate your invitations, even when I refuse them. But sometimes it's hard to do something I love when I feel nothing at all. So please don't push me too hard, trying to tell me, "you used to love this." Because I know, and I still do. And someday, when my depression has loosened its grip on me, I will return to doing what I love. Because the things I like are still the things I like. Because I am not my depression, and my depression is not me.

I am still me. If I cared about you before, then I still care about you now. Even if it may not seem like it. And I am so sorry that sometimes it may seem that way. Truly, I wish that my depression didn't affect you the way I know it does. But I want you to know that that is the depression, not me. I still care. I am sorry that I may ask to be left alone when you are trying your best to reach out to me, or when I refuse to go out and socialize with you when you just want to enjoy my company. I am so sorry if I make you feel that you are insignificant or don't matter to me. I will try my best so you don't feel that way. Because it's not true and you do still matter to me.

I just ask for patience. Patience while I fight my way through this. And I promise I will try my hardest to return to your si Because if I cared about you before, then I care about you now. Because I am not my depression, and my depression is not me.

To You Who Don't Understand,

Sincerely,
Someone Who Wishes You Understood (if only even a little)

Part Two: Losing Control

To You Who Don't Understand,

I'm Tired

Enough. I've had enough.
I can't take much more.
My mind is clouded,
My heart is heavy,
My body cripples under the weight.
How much longer must I carry this burden?
How much further must I walk this treacherous path?
I try in vain to drop this hardship,
To switch onto a different track.
But the burden remains yoked to me,
And there's nowhere else to go.
Why is it me?
Why must I continue to bare these afflictions?
Why must I follow this beaten path?
I'm tired.

Acrostic Poem

Please, can you not see it?
Look at me
Everyone around me going about as if everything is fine
Alone and broken, I stand waiting
Suffocating
Everything around me blurs and fades away

Some sort of release, I need
Afflictions and melancholy burden me
Victim of the demons in my mind
Even my body feels heavy

My life hangs in the balance
Exhausted

To You Who Don't Understand,

Crimson River

Release. Numbness.

I lay in bed staring at my bedroom ceiling. The popcorn texture creates random images from the shadows and sunlight across the ceiling. The constant fluctuating of light continually changes the image's appearance, creating an endless supply of imaginings. This time I see images of mountains and rivers and turtles. And bunnies. Why is it always bunnies? I watch the soft light peeking through my red window curtains, shifting the shadows halfway across this popcorn ceiling, my only indication of the passage of time.

The nothingness is suffocating. I can't pull away from it. It follows me wherever I go, whatever I do. I can't escape it. I can't control it. There's a battle raging on in my mind. A battle I'm slowly losing. Why can't anyone hear me silently screaming? Noise is unbearable but the silence is suffocating.

The pain in my forearm prickles. I gaze at the yellow

X-Acto knife still in my hand. Dark red stains the edge of the blade. How long have I been lying here like this? Did I fall asleep at all? I stare at the red steaks across my arm, now a dark shade of burgundy since drying. I miss the crimson red, the freshness of new blood drawn. The beauty of it with its calming effect. The drops freeze in place at the edge of my arm. Like time stops just for me. Hanging in limbo. Away from reality. The drops that fell from my arm create a red splatter pattern across the bottom of my pyjama shirt. Another article of clothing stained red.

Maybe this life isn't for everybody.

I hear the dull buzzing of my parent's alarm clock in the next room. Time to face another day. Time to clean myself up before my mother comes to my room to wake me for school. Time to go through the motions again. I grab a tissue from my bedside table and wipe the red off the silver blade before throwing it into my drawer. I pick up fresh white gauze and skin tape from the little box in my drawer before forcing myself to the bathroom.

Making sure the door is locked behind me, I let the cool tap water run over my arm. The clear water turns a pinkish red. The cold stings the lines written down my arm. Wrapping the snow white gauze to cover the red, I secure it in place with tape before picking up my toothbrush and brushing my teeth. I finish getting ready for school, throwing on my oversized uniform sweater to hide the bandage.

To You Who Don't Understand,

At school I walk around the hallways with the smile I've perfected. The tinge of pain in my arm a constant reminder of the battle I just fought.

Did I win or lose?

"Aren't you hot in your sweater?" Tom jokes in mock exaggeration.

"Coco's always cold!" my friend Eileen says with a laugh.

I laugh with them, thankful for the hundredth time that my body can't regulate temperature like the average person. That me wearing a sweater in the warm weather is nothing new or out of place. I go through my morning as usual, moving seamlessly from class to class. And then it happened in English class.

"Hey," my friend Steven leans over and whispers above Mr. Peter's explanation of, A Tale of Two Cities. "You ok?"

I turn to him questioningly, "Yeah, why?"

He points at my arm. I look down. My green uniform sleeves are still pulled down, even covering most of my hands. Just how I like it. I look back at him blankly.

"I saw the bandage. Are you ok?" he insists.

"Oh that," I answer flippantly, "Yeah I'm fine."

"What happened?"

"I just hurt myself. You know me, I'm a clutz."

"Okay. Well, be careful. You'll kill yourself one day!"

Before I can form a response, Mr. Peter throws a piece of chalk in our direction.

"Anything you want to share with the class? Maybe it's some wonderful insight into the character of Sidney Carton?"

Steven and I shake our heads silently. Mr. Peter begins talking again. We both glance at each other and smirk.

Steven leans towards me again and whispers, "I'm here if you ever need anything."

I turn to him, "Thanks," I mouth silently and flash him what I hope is my perfected smile.

I spend the rest of the day keeping myself awake in class or chilling in the hallways with my friends. The tinge of pain in my arm dims from distractions, yet I wait to get back home. To get back to the safety of my room, my bed. The battle in my mind is much more tiring when trying to fight it with a smile. By the end of the day the need to control some aspect of my life comes back. To have control over something I feel.

I want to stop. I tell myself over and over again that this is the last time. That I don't need to anymore. But with every cut I can feel the nothingness seep out of my mind and fade from my heart. I have to cut out places for the pain to bleed from. Kill pain with pain.

I can't breathe. Every beat of my heart takes me closer to the edge. I stand precariously at the precipice of a sweet abyss. Ready to jump. Ready to fall. To be taken away. The clicks of the X-Acto knife bring the blade closer. I press the cool metal against my warm skin. My heart pounds, the pulse knows the tip of the blade before the cut. I inhale deeply

To You Who Don't Understand,

before pushing the metal into my arm, the blood rushes to greet its serrated edge. The crimson river flows.

    Release. Numbness.

The World Goes Black

The world goes black,
Then blacker still.
I'm floating in the abyss.
The only thing here,
Pain
And no escape.

To You Who Don't Understand,

Break Free

And she looks up to the sky as she cries out
"Please save me"
When all the chains that bind her to this earth
And her soul calls out for release
She spreads her wings to break free
Can't break free

Time stops in a vortex haze where she stands
Forget it all
The darkness seeps to the depth of her mind
Like a shadow forever cleaved
The demon follows her behind
Can't break free
Can't break free

Don't Take It Personally

To You Who Don't Understand,

Please don't take it personally. We understand that the things we say sometimes affect you. We understand that our actions sometimes upset you. We understand that our emotions sometimes distress you. But please, don't take it personally.

Because as much as we don't want this to affect you, we know that it does, so please know that sometimes the battle is hard to deal with. And we might not always treat you the way you deserve. We might push you away. But please know it doesn't mean we want you to go away. Please don't go away. It may take some time, but please, don't take it personally.

In return, we'll try not to take things personally. We'll try to understand when you don't have the time to talk to us. We'll try to understand that not everything you do is in direct retaliation to us. We'll try to understand when you don't have the patience to deal with all our

To You Who Don't Understand,

emotions at the moment. We'll try not to read too deep into everything.

Because we know we need to remind ourselves that, just like we sometimes need time to myself, so do you. And we know that having to help someone with depression can be a lot for anyone to deal with. So if you need to be away from us for a while, we will try to understand. And we will be waiting for you when you're ready again. Just like we hope you would wait for us.

So please, try not to take everything personally and in return, we will try not to take things personally too.

Sincerely,

Someone Who Wishes You Understood (if only even a little)

Never to Forget

Frustrated these thoughts won't leave me alone
A mirage from the that comes to get me
And draws me in to an endless void
From which I can't escape
And never to forget, never to forget

I've taken my stroll down memory lane
And I'm lost in its forest of dreams
And endless fog clouds my way of escape
Can't find my way back to reality
And never to forget, never to forget

In this world from whence I came
My place, no more to find
Everything seems so surreal
But it is impossible to turn back
And never to forget, never to forget

To You Who Don't Understand,

    Inside I've cried those endless tears
    I've slowly been washed away
    The fire of life that once burned bright
    Is now extinguished and only a scar remains
    And never to forget, never to forget

    I feel no more
    Barred the floodgates of emotions
    But reminiscence washes over me
    I'm drowning in the past
    And never to forget, never to forget

    I want to scream and throw a fit
    To get this off my mind
    But I realize it won't ever be gone
    For its deep within my soul
    And never to forget, never to forget

The Pain

The pain slices like a knife

Constricting my heart so that I can't breathe

Like my soul is being wretched from my body

Silently I lie back in darkness

Unable to move

Unable to fight

Feeling the knife stab with every beat of my heart

Concentrating on my slow and ragged breaths

I wait for it to pass…

To You Who Don't Understand,

Castle of Blankets

The first rays of morning brightness find their way through my red curtains, casting a bloody haze over everything in my room. The only indication that the darkness of night has passed. But my darkness continues. I lie curled up in my bed in a fetal position, underneath the protection of my hand-me-down comforter - praying to be safe in my little castle of blankets. But there's no where I can hide from myself. There is nowhere to run from the demons in my mind that threaten to destroy me. That seep energy from my body making it difficult to move. To breathe.

I go through the long list of things I should tackle today. Finish final essays. Study for exams. Do laundry. Clean my overcrowded room. Call my doctor, again. I need to do these things. My mind knows I need to get them done. School is always a priority for me, how else would I be able to keep my grades up and get accepted into grad school?

But not today.

Today, nothing matters.

Not the fact that I have several big research essays to finish. Not the fact that final examinations start next week. Not the fact that my dirty laundry pile is overflowing or that my clean laundry is strewn across my floor. Not the fact that I am about a week late booking a follow-up appointment with my doctor. Not even the fact that I got into a fight with my boyfriend and we still haven't talked properly since then.

Nothing.

None of it matters.

And I know that all of it matters, most of it matters a lot, but I just can't bring myself to care. I don't even care about the fact that I know later I will regret not caring.

I should probably eat. I can't take my anti-inflammatory pills or pain medications on an empty stomach. I sit up a little and lean against my pillow. My limbs feel heavy. Hoisting my body up leaves me breathless. The prospect of getting out of bed and making food tires me out. I lie back down and pull the comforter up to my chin. I skip the food. And my medications.

My phone vibrates on my bedside table. I glance over. Fourteen unanswered messages and three missed calls since the last time I bothered to check. I click the clear notifications button before putting my phone down, messages unread and calls unreturned. Right now, just the thought of talking to someone, anyone, exhausts me. Another thing added to my

To You Who Don't Understand,

list of things to do: apologize to my boyfriend, best friend, and cousins for ignoring them. Somewhere in the back of my mind a tiny voice tells me again that it's not worth it, that I should care. I should pick up the phone and answer them, maybe even reach out for help. But I don't. That voice isn't loud enough. And I can't get myself to care enough.

I lay in my bed staring at nothing. My eyes are open, but unfocused. I see shapes and colours but nothing else. Nothing else matters. I listen to the beat of my heart. Feel the dull ache with every pounding of my chest. Telling me I'm still alive. I'm still here. I lay in pseudo-silence. I'm sure there are sounds around me. Birds and squirrels are always outside my window. Someone tinkering around in the kitchen before they go to work. Or after they're done work. Maybe I even left my playlist on from last night when I tried to listen to music. But I hear nothing. My world has grown silent. I don't know how long I lay in bed, unmoving. I lay in this pseudo-silent world of shapes and colours where time does not exist.

My mother shatters this world when she opens my bedroom door and steps in. She looks at me. The whites of her eyes become more visible.

"You're still home? In bed?"

I just look at her blankly for a moment or two before nodding. She looks around my room and then back at my helpless state. She shakes her head. I don't swing this low that often, but she knows the signs when she sees them. She says nothing about it.

"Well I just got home and I'm making supper now. Do you want some?"

I don't want any. I don't want anything. Or to do anything. I have no appetite. The thought of food doesn't appeal to me. I shake my head.

"Have you taken your medicine?"

I shake my head again.

"Well you need to take your medicine. No wonder you can't move. I'll make you some food, make sure you eat it. Then take your medicine."

My mother turns to leave the room, but she faces me one last time, "You need to get out of bed anak. This isn't good for you."

With that she leaves and shuts the door behind her. The light from my window has dimmed, leaving my room in dark shadows. I didn't realize the day had gone by until now. I fight with my mind to get up. To do something, anything, so that my day isn't wasted. So that I will not have spent another day, and the better portion of my week, curled up in bed making no progress with my life. I fight with my mind to care about something, anything. But I can't make myself. I continue to lie in bed.

I try to daydream. Daydreaming is one of my favourite hobbies. An escape from my reality, even when I know my

To You Who Don't Understand,

life isn't so bad. I get caught up in so many different worlds I have playing out in my head. Sometimes I even get lost in them, unable to distinguish reality from daydream. But those are often the best ones. The ones that feel so real I could swear they were more of a memory from a past life than just a figment of my imagination. Sometimes I can force myself to enter a daydream, other times they come to me out of nowhere and I just surrender myself to the fantasy. But today, no daydreams come. Today, even my mind is too barren to save me.

One thing. Just get one thing done. I force myself to sit up against my pillow. I breathe deeply. Picking up my phone I search through my contacts for Dr. Penchav. I press dial and hold the phone to my ear. The secretary's voice breaks the fourth ring. After several minutes I hang up the phone, with an appointment to meet my doctor in three days at 10:00 A.M. It may not seem like much, but on days like today, it's the small accomplishments that matter. That's more than I've accomplished all week. I lie back in bed. Maybe tomorrow I'll be able to get out of bed and go to class.

Erosion

Depression kills. Not in a cancerous way that relentlessly destroys your cells, but rather in the steady erosion of self.

To You Who Don't Understand,

I Don't Want to Feel Anymore

I don't want to feel anymore

Please

Just stop

The tears that wet my eyes and cheeks

The salty taste on my lips

What can I do to stop this pain?

My heart entangled in thorns

Squeezing tighter

Piercing

Just cut right through

And squeeze to death

Please

I don't want to feel anymore

Second Chance

My cheek felt cold from the laminate tile on the bathroom floor. Tears flow freely down my face. There was no one here to see me. I was alone. I was cold. I was tired. Tired of everything in this life. Tired of fighting to keep afloat.

I didn't have a plan. There was no elaborate plot to end my suffering. I just knew that I needed out. I took the rest of my sleeping pills in one shot. I followed it with half a bottle of Ibuprofen. I choked the pills down, one by one, two by two. I curled up on the bathroom floor with the empty bottle still in my hand.

I hadn't anticipated the gut-wrenching hurt that coursed through my body. I clutched my head between my hands and tried to block the deafening ring echoing through my skull. My vision blurred. I cried against the penetrating ache that I felt in my heart. Or was it my stomach?

My mind swam. The floor shifted underneath me and the

room tilted. The world spun on a different axis. I swallowed with difficulty, trying to push back the saliva forming in my mouth. My mind dipped in and out through waves of nausea. I tried to focus on the garbage bin in the corner but it ran away from my sight. The muscles in my stomach contracted. I crawled across the cold bathroom floor and stuck my head in the toilet, barely before the vomit flowed. The medicine, my last meal, bile, blood, and everything else came up and out, until I thought for sure I would throw up whatever life I had left in my body. Time blurred.

Convulsions came. I collapsed to the floor. Panic seeped in with the pain. I clutched my knees to my chest. I lay limp on the cold floor. Muscle spasms shook my entire body.

Was dying really as painful as living? I didn't know which I preferred. My heart pounded. It palpitated so fast it felt like my heart would collapse inward.

My breath caught in my lungs. Gasping for air sent waves of pain over my body. I tried to breathe in deeply but I couldn't get any oxygen.

This was it. If I couldn't breathe anymore, this must be it.

Terror gripped me.

I realized I wanted to live. Tears stung my face. I lay exhausted on the cold laminate floor. I prayed. I cried and begged and prayed. I promised God that if he let me live I would treasure every moment. I cried out to the God that I had forgotten.

Time passed and I breathed rough gasps.

Time passed and my heart beat steadied into an uneven deep thudding.

Time passed and the sharp convulsions became a soft shaking.

Time passed and the hurt dulled.

Time passed. And I was still here. I felt weak but still here.

Part Three: Learning to Cope

Fly with Me to Neverland

I've heard of a wondrous place
Well beyond time and space
It's a mystical land
Where everything is grand
From the brightest stars to green crisp leaves
Everything will be just as you please
So, won't you take my hand
And fly with me to Neverland

All these thoughts in my head
I just can't get to bed
Thoughts of school and romance
And my lack of a chance
To go anywhere in life
Without running into strife
So, won't you take my hand
And fly with me to Neverland

To You Who Don't Understand,

>I can't stand it, I've had enough
>I used to think I was so tough
>Now I'm drowning in my tears and pain
>And wish to never breath again
>So don't you see that I must leave
>And head for this place where I won't grieve
>So please, won't you take my hand
>And fly with me to Neverland

Mary

I sit in the corner of the large, sterile room. The place looks almost like the nursing homes I used to visit with my grandpa when we would volunteer to sing. A few old televisions hang from the ceiling, playing old movies that no one really pays attention to. There are rows of cracked, pleather-lined chairs scattered around the room. They sit in between random circle tables with stools attached to the bottom. Everything in here is bolted down.

A girl around my age dances across an empty spot on the floor in her light blue hospital gown. Short, dark hair bounces around her face. Her eyes are closed as she listens to the music only she can hear. It's relaxing to watch her. Better than watching the old man who sits on a chair rocking back and forth in the middle of the room. I try to hear the music she hears as she twirls around.

The girl stops dancing. She stands, unmoving and eyes closed. Before I can speculate on what she'll do next, she

To You Who Don't Understand,

crumples to the floor like a listless puppet whose strings had just been cut. I look around the room wondering where all the nurses went. Maybe she is just tired, her body languid from all the dancing. Her slim figure lying on the white tiled floor. Eyes still closed, her arms begin to flail, mimicking the action of the breaststroke. Then she stops again.

She lies on the floor like a corpse, pale and lifeless, legs bent at a slight angle, arms out to her sides. A nurse walks right by her without giving her a second glance, instead hurrying to the guy across the room who was scraping the wall with his pointer finger. Her eyes flutter open. She stares at the ceiling before slowly rising to a sitting position. A look of confusion is etched on her face as her eyes wander around the room.

Her eyes meet mine for the first time. She cocks her head slightly and stands to her feet. I lower my eyes. With slow, steady steps she walks towards me. I sink further into my chair and cross my arms.

"Hi, I'm Mary."

Her bubbly voice doesn't match the placid look on her face. I look at her, hoping my body language deters her from any further conversation. She sits in the seat next to me.

"What's your name?"

"Coco." I give her my nickname.

Her face breaks into a smile as she lets out a small giggle. She grabs my forearm with her wiry hands.

"Oh thank goodness! You came after all."

"Um... what?"

I try to pry my arm away but her grip hardens. Still smiling, her dark eyes stare into me. The smile doesn't reach her eyes. Nothing reaches her eyes.For the second time today, she reminds me of a puppet.

She leans in close. "You see, they told me you would come."

"Uh, who told you?"

I try to scoot over in my chair as far away as I can from her. I glance around the room looking for somebody who could help.

"They did, of course."

She looks me squarely in the eyes, the darkness of her eyes turning a shade blacker.

Her voice drops to a whisper, "I can save you."

A nurse saves me the trouble of replying when she fetches me for my appointment with Dr. Wersner. I follow her out of the sterile room, glancing back just in time to see Mary break her stare from me to close her eyes. She begins dancing again.

Inside the doctor's office I sit in a large, plush armchair while I twist and untwist my fingers, waiting for Dr. Wersner to speak.

"In my opinion, it's ok for you to be going home, as long as you have some sort of support at home, which you've told

To You Who Don't Understand,

me you do. I think there are much sicker people here than you.

    I think of Mary. "Ya, I think so too."

Some Advice to Help

To You Who Don't Understand,

Because sometimes it's difficult to know what to do when someone you love suffers from depression. Because sometimes you feel powerless as you watch someone you love spiral downward. Because sometimes it's frustrating and scary to have no idea what you can do to help. I write this letter to you. Please listen to my words. Maybe you can help me.

Please, listen. Just listen. We don't need lectures, we don't need lessons. But having someone there to listen when we have things we want to say can help relieve our affliction. Just sharing with someone can lighten the heavy burden we carry - even if you don't know what to say. And if we're not ready to talk, then don't push us. Even lying next to us in silence can help give us rest.

Please, realize that treatment is key. It's not just going to fade away and we won't just grow out of it one day. It's a part of us now, and we are having to learn to fight

To You Who Don't Understand,

it in our own way. Depression is an illness, and medical care can work to heal us. To help us cope. If you notice we may need treatment, then maybe we can accept that we may need help.

Please, stay in contact. I understand this may be difficult. We sometimes isolate ourselves so we don't bother you. We sometimes don't have the energy to communicate with you. We sometimes have no will to have any form of contact at all. So you may have to work extra hard to support and engage us. But it's one of the best things you can do for us. Be there.

Please, help us focus on small goals. When every day we go into a battle with our mind, recognition for little accomplishments can boost our moral. Things that you may take for granted, like getting out of bed, can be a huge achievement for us. We try to get through little by little, day by day. Help us by encouraging and praising us in all the small things we do.

Please, be informed. Trying to understand depression shows that you're trying your best to understand us. There are articles everywhere speaking about depression. Being informed can help you respond better to things we're going through. I know that most people don't find it fun to study, but what if it can help save us? We're doing everything we can to fight this and it's always better to be informed and prepared if you're going to battle alongside us. And this is a battle.

Please, pay attention. We won't always cry out for help. Not because we don't want to but often we can't or don't remember how. Sometimes we get so focused on fighting our battles that we forget the world around us - including the people around who want to help. And sometimes we want to hide the hurt we feel. But if you are paying attention, you'll see when we need you most.

Sincerely,

Someone Who Wishes You Understood (if only even a little)

To You Who Don't Understand,

Enough

Why do things happen the way they do?

I wasn't able to give you the world. But I gave you my world. I guess it wasn't enough.

Nothing was ever enough.

You needed more money. More things. More time.

Always just a little bit more.

But what about me?

You wanted more from me. But I never had anymore.

Because I already gave you my everything. I guess it wasn't enough.

Nothing was ever enough.

If I could turn back time and redo things I still wouldn't know what to do.

Should have… could have… would have…

But I did everything I knew how to do. And more. I guess it still wasn't enough.

Nothing was ever enough.

Now I've had to let you go. And I never knew I could do that.

But I had to. And I did.

And I hope now you can find someone who is enough. Enough for you.

Because maybe, just maybe, it wasn't me who wasn't enough.

Maybe my enough was just never going to fit your enough.

And I'm still learning. And growing.

But maybe my enough will fit with someone else's enough.

And I pray that you find someone else whose enough fits your enough.

Because you deserve the world.

And I just couldn't give it to you.

So now I've let you go.

To You Who Don't Understand,

How to Choose Your Words Wisely Pt.1

To You Who Don't Understand,

Because I understand that sometimes knowing what to say to the person you love who lives with depression is not easy. You may be scared to say something wrong and make matters worse. We know you mean well when you try to encourage us, but sometimes what you say are things we really don't need to hear. We understand that our life might not be so bad. But sometimes the demons in our head cloud our judgement and make us feel otherwise. And that is why we fight. Everyday. To remind ourselves that life is not that bad. So I write this letter to you, to help you choose your words wisely. And so here's a list of things we'd like you to try and avoid saying to us.

"Lots of people live with less than you, you have no right to be depressed, you should be thankful." - This is a sure-fire way to make us feel a lot worse. We can logically understand better than anyone that there are people who are worse off than ourselves. Yet that doesn't stop us from feeling this way. If you want to get a little scientific, the serotonin levels in our brain don't care about our situation in life, and it's the serotonin in our brain (or lack thereof) that can make us feel the way we do.

"You have a [boyfriend/girlfriend, job, kids, husband/wife], you have nothing to be depressed about." - Another certain way to make us feel worse. We understand that we have people in our lives who love us unconditionally. And we really appreciate it, you have no idea how much it actually means to us. But again, this kind of comment makes it seem like the blame about how we feel is on us, rather than outside (or technically inside) circumstances.

"You don't pray enough." - First of all, who are you to judge what enough prayer is? There are days when we can pray non-stop throughout the whole day and it doesn't mean we're any less depressed. In fact, if we believe in prayer enough to be praying, then it is probably prayer that is getting us through the day. You telling us that we don't pray enough can make us feel belittled and not good enough. What if we are praying with all our might, and yet we still feel this way? What then?

"You just have to keep busy." - Our depression is not just something we can choose to ignore. It is something that affects us deeply, emotionally and physically. Keeping

To You Who Don't Understand,

our minds busy can help at times, but it doesn't work to permanently erase the depression from our minds and body. Telling us to keep ourselves busy can mean you think we are suffering because we are focusing on our depression, and if we just focus on something else we'll feel better. This can make us feel like we are to blame for our own suffering.

"But you're always smiling and seem so happy, there's no way you can be depressed." - Just because we smile doesn't mean we're ok. Smiling can be practiced. People with depression aren't the only ones to use it as a mask. When you're upset at something your boss did at work, will you still not smile to their face to hide how you really feel? Sometimes we don't want the world to judge or question, so we cover our pain with a smile.

"It's all in your head." - This statement again puts the blame of how we feel all on us. But first let me say that yes, though it may start in our heads, depression affects every aspect of our lives. We feel real, physical pain as a result. And this is not an imaginary pain that we make up. It's real. And it hurts. The fatigue we feel is very real. It is difficult to move through simple daily tasks. Even if it's "all in our heads," the pain is very real.

Sincerely,

Someone Who Wishes You Understood (if even only a little)

You Are You

You are you
You are nobody else
You are not who others tell you you are
Or what they tell you you should be

You are you
You are not your father
Or your family name
Or the expectations they have of you

Be who you want to be
Do what you want to do
Live how you want to live

You are you, you are nobody else
You are you
And you are something wonderful

To You Who Don't Understand,

My Prayer, My Plea

I stand before you now
Broken
So I give up my spirit to you
I can do no more without you
I surrender everything to you
Take my life and make it yours
No more fighting
Let your judgement pass
Reveal your plan to me
My life belongs to you
Take my selfish desires
And form them to your will
My spirit is too weak
To continue this life without you
And so I proclaim now,
My life, my future, my spirit
All lie in your hands

Battles

The battle is not won when we 'get over' our depression. The battle is won when we continue to wake up every morning ready to fight our demons.

To You Who Don't Understand,

How to Choose Your Words Wisely Pt.2

To You Who Don't Understand,

It's difficult to know what to say and what not to say when speaking to someone suffering from depression. You may say something with good intentions but your words may not have the good affect you were intending. We appreciate it, but please understand that many things you say out of concern, can have the opposite effect on our moral. So I write this letter to you. Here's another list of more phrases we'd like you to try and avoid saying to us.

"Don't sleep all the time. Go do something you enjoy."
- It's not that easy. We don't just wake up and decide that maybe we'll stay in bed all day and do nothing. This might seem relaxing to some people but usually it's anything but relaxing for us. We're stuck in bed with our thoughts. And when I say stuck, I mean stuck. Like anyone who suffers from the flu or something chronic like an autoimmune disease, extreme fatigue and body

pain are symptoms, just as they are for a person with depression. Sometimes it's not that we don't want to get out of bad, sometimes it's that we can't. Please just be patient.

"But you're too [smart, funny, pretty, successful, etc] to be depressed." - If you do say this, thank you for the compliment, but please understand that our depression doesn't depend on outside factors of our personality, appearance or overall life. It's something internal. A struggle that is generally beyond factors, though yes some circumstances in life can be triggers. It's worth noting that sometimes depression will constantly tell us the exact opposite of whatever compliment you are giving us. That we are stupid, or ugly or a failure.

"You don't need medication, it's not like you're really sick." - Unfortunately, depression is an illness just like any other. The ailments we feel are real, the afflictions we feel are real. It's not just something we can 'turn off'. Believe me, if we could, we would. When someone really suffers from depression it's not enjoyable, and we definitely don't do it for the attention. And sometimes medications can help. It doesn't mean that we are any less of a person for taking something that helps suppress our ailments. Now, not everyone is the same. Some don't want to take medications and that's fine too. Please respect our doctor's opinions and our own choices. You wouldn't deny a cancer patient their treatment, why is ours any different?

To You Who Don't Understand,

"It will pass."/ "You'll get over it." - Yes, this "episode" will probably pass, hopefully, eventually. But depression is not something we will "get over eventually". For many of us, we will fight this for the better portion of our lives. And likely we've been fighting this for quite a while already. So you telling us that "it will pass" and "we'll get over it" sounds like a lie. We're thinking, "Yes, but when? Because I'm tired already..."

"Just try harder." - When faced with this comment someone close to me said, "You can't just turn on happy like a light switch." I agree, we can't just think ourselves happy, or turn on a switch and automatically feel or not feel a certain way. In fact, many of us are trying. Trying our absolute hardest to get through another day, another hour, another minute. Because depression is not only an illness, it can be a battle. And we are constantly fighting. Fighting for our next breath. If we weren't trying our hardest, we wouldn't be here. Because it's much easier to give up then to keep fighting against yourself every day. And that's the simple truth.

Sincerely,

Someone Who Wishes You Understood (if even only a little)

Office Hours

Tick tock tick tock

The tiny silver clock echoes in the dark silent room. It sits on the round coffee table between us. I shift in the large leather arm chair and the unnatural squeaking of my body against the leather covers the ticking for a second. My butt falls deeper into the overly plush seat. I glance up at the lady sitting across from me. She stares at me from over her red framed glasses. Not smiling, not frowning, just staring. The pen in her hand rests on the lined notepad on her lap. Ready to write. Ready to write about my problems. About my feelings. About what's wrong with me. About me.

Tick tock tick tock

I don't understand why she's just sitting there, staring at me. Am I supposed to talk first? But I don't know what to say. I'm here because Dr. Maclure from the psych ward insisted that it would benefit me. That maybe it could help

To You Who Don't Understand,

me. I didn't want to. I thought that it would permanently stamp the word *mental* across my forehead. But nothing else worked, and I was tired of feeling this way. I wanted to feel better. To feel like myself again. So, I finally agreed to try.

Tick tock tick tock

"So why don't you tell me a little bit about yourself? You're a student?" she asks, finally breaking the silence.

"Ya, I'm a student."

Tick tock tick tock

We sit in silence for another minute. She's probably waiting for me to continue.

I don't.

"What are you studying?" she pushes.

"Um… a little bit of everything. I'm not sure what I want to do with my life yet."

"Ok," she nods and makes a note on her lined notepad.

Tick tock tick tock

I glance at the little silver clock and wonder if this is really what people pay for. To sit here in silence? The clock reads 5:13 P.M. Thirteen minutes into the appointment and all she knows about me is that I am a student studying everything. And what she's seen in my file. I wish I could see the secrets hidden in that file. The notes about the crazy me. About the times, for no reason at all, I lost all desire to live. About the times I had to cut away the pain before it became too much and overtook my sanity. About the times I fought with the demons in my head; thinking I was going completely mental. Is that what she wants me to talk about?

I don't know where to start.

Tick tock tick tock

She sits looking at me. Staring. Expecting something from me. I look away.

"Why don't we start with your childhood?"

I suppress a smile, amused that they really use that line.

"Um, pretty normal, I guess. I still have both parents. One sister, one brother. Both younger than me. Grew up in the church. We were never close to rich, but we had our basic needs met."

Her pen runs furiously as she writes down the mundane details of my average childhood. Maybe there is some special event hidden deep in my ordinary past that had a traumatic effect on my consciousness. Maybe now someone can tell me why I am so broken.

"So, how does that make you feel?"

I pause before answering. Is she asking me how does my entire childhood make me feel? Or some specific aspect of my childhood that I shared?

Tick tock tick tock

She sits staring at me, face unreadable. She probably earned her poker face after years of talking to crazies like me. Except I wasn't crazy, according to the doctor, just mentally ill. If there's a difference.

To You Who Don't Understand,

"I don't know."

"Ok," she says, cocking her head to the side, her eyes still locked on my face, "Why don't we start from the end then. What were you feeling when you tried to end your life?"

Tick Tock Tick Tock

I glance at the clock. 5:39 P.M. Now we're getting to the big stuff. The stuff that really matters. Or maybe it all matters and I haven't figured out how. I force myself to think back on a memory I try to suppress. I can feel my eyes darting around the room, unable to find something to focus on. Her eyes on me, unmoving. She wants to know how I felt? Even I don't know how I felt. All I know is that I felt too much of it. So much that I had to get out. So much that I couldn't breathe.

Tick tock tick tock

"I felt like I was suffocating."

She makes note of my suffocating, or she could be playing tic-tac-toe. Her notepad is aimed away from me. She looks back at me with the same placid face she's had the entire appointment.

"What happened that made you think you were suffocating?"

I think back to the darkest moments of my life. The times when I felt alone, even though I was rarely ever alone. I think about the time when my mind clouded over. To the time I thought I could feel my mind breaking. As if my mind was a flimsy sheet of paper, it effortlessly ripped in two and I could no longer keep my hold on reality.

But I didn't want to tell her this. She'd probably write the word psychotic on her little notepad and then I'd be taken away and locked up in some mental institution. If I could just escape from here. Not just this office, this reality.

"Where did you just go?"

She interrupts my thoughts.

It takes me a second to understand her question. I look at the clock. 5:51 P.M. How long had I been in my own mind? I hadn't even heard the ticking of the time passing.

"Sorry," I say simply, "I like to daydream."

She makes a memo of that in her notebook.

"Well our time is almost up for today," she says, setting the pen down on top of her notepad.

"Ok," I nod.

"This was just an initial meeting, so I could get to know you. I'd like to suggest maybe some cognitive behavioral therapy. It works to help you control your moods and emotions. I think you could benefit from that."

Tick tock tick tock

"But we can talk about it next time. I'd like to see you again, if that's ok?"

"Sure," I shrug.

To You Who Don't Understand,

Will You?

When the world is falling all around me
So everything is black,
And the end is too difficult to see,
Will you still have my back?

When my body cannot withstand much more
From pain I can't express,
And I am covered in blood from the war,
Will you clean up my mess?

When my mind begins to make its attack
From the demons within,
And all of my beliefs begin to crack,
Will you still help me win?

If I hold on to you, will you save me?

"I'm Fine"

To You Who Don't Understand,

If someone you know and love lives with depression, chances are you've heard us say, "I'm fine." Sometimes, you want to check in on us and see how we are doing. Or maybe it's just a casual, "How are you?" Whatever the reason for your asking, please don't always take our answer at face value.

Hidden behind our "I'm fine" is often a world of hurt. Just like it's common phrase as the answer for the greeting exchange of, "How are you?" Sometimes we use "I'm fine" on purpose, because what we're going through is too heavy to explain. Here are some things that we might mean when you hear us say, "I'm fine."

"I'm fine," can mean: "I really don't want to talk about it right now."

"I'm fine," can mean: "Even if I told you how I'm really feeling you probably wouldn't understand, so why

To You Who Don't Understand,

should I bother?"

"I'm fine," can mean: "Please don't believe me when I say I'm fine, please notice my situation."

"I'm fine," can mean: "Please help me."

"I'm fine," can mean: "I have too many things going on in my head at once that I don't even know where to begin."

"I'm fine," can mean: "It doesn't matter."

So, just because we may say "I'm fine" doesn't necessarily mean we are. Sounds complicated, I know. Over time you may be able to tell the subtle differences in our "I'm fine." But for now, please just try to bear with us. After all, we're only human.

Sincerely,

Someone Who Wishes You Understood (if only even a little)

Today is a Good Day

"Auntie Coco! Wake up!"

The weight of my four-year-old goddaughter drops onto my limp, sleeping body at full force. Coughing dramatically, I roll over on my side, pulling her small body down under me. With my arms and legs wrapped tightly around her, I snore loudly.

"Auntie Coco!" Rose giggles wildly and wiggles around in my arms, "Auntie Coco, wake up!"

I wait for a pause in her thrashing before removing my arms from around her and look at her in surprise.

"Rose! Why are you in my bed?!"

"I came to wake you up," Rose can't stop giggling, "Mommy said to come get you."

I pull her down for our usual tickle fight before heading to my best friend's kitchen. The Christmas tree lights are already on and sparkling in the living room.

To You Who Don't Understand,

"Mooooommmm, Auntie Coco is awake now!" Rose dances into the room before me.

Selene takes in my appearance before throwing her head back in laughter, "Morning babes."

"How does she have so much energy in the morning!" I flop into the seat next to my boyfriend, "Am I the last one up?"

Maru kisses me on my forehead, "Nah baby, we just got up."

"Tom and Elizabeth just left with Sierra, they say bye." Selene informs me.

"Damn they left already? Why didn't anybody wake me?"

"Partied too hard last night eh?" Jace, Selene's husband, teases me.

"I had a rough few weeks," I say with feign insult, "Exams killed me."

I think back to just a few weeks ago when I was stuck in bed. Back when nothing mattered to me, not even the exams that killed me. Back when I was stuck in my castle of blankets. Back when the hospital put me on suicide watch and made me fill out a daily questionnaire to track my depression.

"What should we do today?" Maru asks me.

I turn to him, feeling a genuine smile burst forth from inside me. Today my black shadow doesn't feel so close.

"Anything!"

A confused smile forms as he furrows his eyebrows.

Selene laughs as she flips an egg on the stove.

I laugh and try again, "Well, Selene and I want to go Christmas shopping at the Niagara Outlets. It's like six minutes away."

Collapsing onto Selene's plush couch, I hang my legs over the side of the armrest. Selene flops next to me and swings her arms up with a dramatic sigh. Rose jumps across both of us, playing with her new toy.

"How much money did you win again, Maru?" Jace asks.

He walks into the living room and dumps the armful of shopping bags from earlier today.

"A hundred bucks."

"Pretty good for his first time at a casino, no?" I chime in.

"Ya, but that's how they catch you. You win a bit so you keep going back, then lose thousands!" Jace jokes.

"Nah," Maru says confidently, "it was fun but I probably still won't go much. But it did help to pay off her new purse."

I smile at him but before I can reply Rose jumps back on my lap, her new stuffed animal already forgotten, squished in between the cushions of the couch.

"Auntie Coco! Wanna watch the princess movie?"

"Ok," I laugh, "let's watch it.

I pull her into my arms as Maru takes his seat beside me.

To You Who Don't Understand,

Jace walk up to the television to set up Netflix while Selene gets up to reheat some of last night's Christmas dinner. I fall back into Maru's chest with a sigh.

Today is a good day.

Living with Depression

To You Who Might Understand (even if momentarily)

Take a breath. Close your eyes and just breathe. Take a moment to yourself. Steady your pulse, slow your heart beat. It helps. And it will get better, I promise.

They may not be able to "help you" the way you think they should. Helping someone who lives with depression is a monumental task. Hey, if it were easy don't you think we could just help ourselves? It can be even more difficult for someone who doesn't understand because they don't know where to begin to help.

Some advice: reach out. I know, scary right? It may seem like you're in this, but there is. There is always someone. A family member, a friend, a guidance counsellor, a help line... There is always someone. They may not always understand what you're going through, but please be patient. It's difficult for them too. And remember sometimes you don't actually need someone who understands, you just need someone who wants to

To You Who Don't Understand,

be there for you.

And it's not necessarily about "getting over it," it's more about getting through it. Recognize that sometimes symptoms can hit for no reason at all, and that is not your fault! Sometimes, it's just about the chemical imbalances in your brain. And it's a benefit to have people around who want to help - even if they don't exactly understand what you're dealing with.

I also understand the feeling of sometimes just wanting to be alone. Somedays we just need our space, to breathe, to think. But I also know from experience that sometimes just having someone around, even if the both of you are doing nothing at all, it can help. Especially during times those feelings of 'alone-ness'. So don't shut them out just because they don't understand. They will never understand if you don't let them try.

It's scary to think that the first step to 'healing' might actually start with you. But they can't help if you don't let them. And I think it's time that we all start trying to heal. Depression may be something you have to live with for the rest of your lives, but it doesn't need to consume us.

As someone much wiser once told me, don't live IN your depression, learn to live WITH it.

Sincerely,
Someone Who Does Understand

To You Who Don't Understand,

Acknowledgements

First, to my Lord and Heavenly Father, my saving grace.

To Papa and Mama, for all the love and support you gave me my whole life. I wouldn't be where I am today without your constant sacrifices and guidance.

To Professor Guy Allen, for all the encouragement and advice given, not just with my book but throughout my university career. You are an inspiration and I am so glad you pushed me to get this book done.

To Ate Em, for all the [often last minute] editing. And because you do matter. This book wouldn't have happened without you.

To Ate Sar, for the information and recommendations on what to include in the book. Your opinions were helpful and important to me.

To Takayuki, for troubleshooting just about every technical problem I came across (which was alot!), helping with the cover design and supporting me through this whole overwhelming process. I can't thank you enough.

To Kaykay, for driving me to school all the time and giving "gentle" advice on time management. You're the best little-big sister I could've asked for.

To Jojo-boy, for helping me order my required texts online, getting all my mail, and always fixing the darn printer. You're an awesome, not-so-baby brother.

To my editing group: Karina, Amber, Jen and Anne. Thank you for all the crazy editing sessions and great suggestions. We did it!

To my copy editor, Jade , for all the constructive criticism and positive encouragement. You were a delight to work with.

To Maiko-san, for the amazing artwork for my cover. You are so talented! (And to Nagisa-chan, for the hook-up!)

To all my other friends and family, who have helped me by reading a story or two, or encouraging me one way or another. Just because I haven't mentioned you by name doesn't mean I don't know what you've done, and just know I appreciate it all!

www.ingramcontent.com/pod-product-compliance
Lightning Source LLC
Chambersburg PA
CBHW051346040426
42453CB00007B/434